Which W

written by John Lockyer

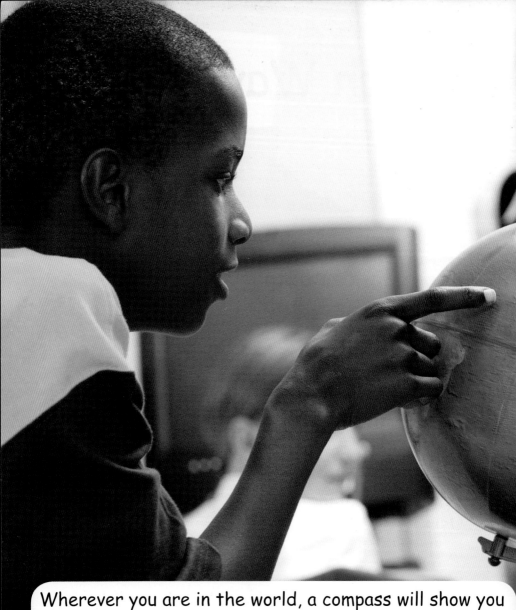

Wherever you are in the world, a compass will show you which way you are going. Whichever way you turn, you will face one direction. It will be somewhere between north, south, east and west.

North is the direction that faces the North Pole. South, which is the opposite of north, is the direction to the South Pole. The direction to the right is called east and the direction to the left is called west.

When you don't have a map, you can use a compass to help you find your way. A compass has a magnetic needle that always points north. It points north because it is pulled by strong magnetic forces at the North Pole.

When the needle points to N for north, it is easy to see which way is south and east and west.

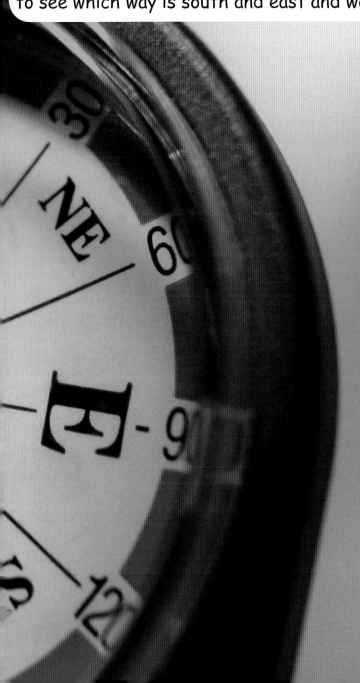

Darwi

Perth

The four main directions are often used to name the parts of a country. The four parts of Africa are North Africa, South Africa, East Africa and West Africa.

The compass can help you to find cities in a country. In Australia, Darwin is north, Melbourne is south, Sydney is east, and Perth is west.

Sydney

Melbourne

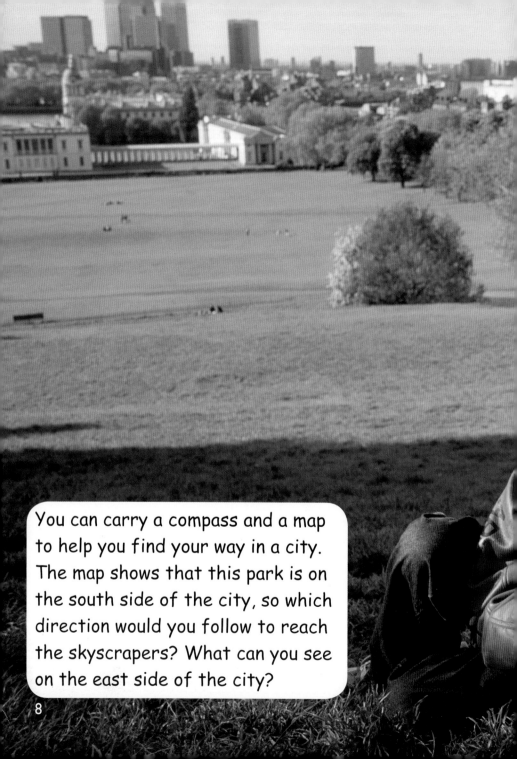

You can carry a compass and a map to help you find your way in a city. The map shows that this park is on the south side of the city, so which direction would you follow to reach the skyscrapers? What can you see on the east side of the city?

In this school, the sports track is on the east side. The soccer field is north, the classrooms are south, but what is west?

Where is the road? Which way are the cars facing? Which way would you go to play on the tennis courts?

Jessie has made a map that shows some of the things she can see from her home. If she looks north she can see the school.

What can she see to the east of the school?
What can she see to the west of her home?
Which way is the blue car going?

You should always carry a compass when you are hiking. In the woods, there are rivers, hills, and lots of trees. It would be easy to get lost without a compass to show you which way to go.

When you are sailing, a compass is useful. At sea, everything looks the same. There are no roads or signs to show you where to go. A compass will help you to find land safely.

You can use a compass in fog, in the dark, or even in a blizzard, when the snow makes it hard to see where you are going. With a compass, you will always be able to find the right way.